Ships and Seafarers

Rosemary Rees
Sue Styles
Adam Hook

HEINEMANN

Heinemann Educational
a division of Heinemann Publishers
(Oxford) Ltd
Halley Court, Jordan Hill, Oxford OX2 8EJ

OXFORD LONDON EDINBURGH MADRID
ATHENS BOLOGNA PARIS MELBOURNE
SYDNEY AUCKLAND SINGAPORE TOKYO
IBADAN NAIROBI HARARE GABORONE
PORTSMOUTH NH (USA)

© Rosemary Rees, Sue Styles, Adam Hook 1993

The moral right of the proprietors has been asserted

First published 1993

98 97 96 95 94 93
10 9 8 7 6 5 4 3 2 1

British Library Cataloguing in publication data is available from the British Library on request.

ISBN 0 435 04261 0

Designed by Ron Kamen, Green Door Design Ltd, Basingstoke, Hants
Printed in Spain by Mateu Cromo

Acknowledgements
The authors and publisher would like to thank the following for permission to reproduce photographs:

Arxiu MAS: 4.2C
Barnaby's Picture Library: 7H
British Library: 1B, 8.1A
British Library/Bridgeman Art Library: 7F
Trustees of the British Museum: 1A, 2C
J. Allan Cash Photo Library: 7I
Peter Clayton: 2B
Dagli Orti: 7D
C. M. Dixon: 3.1A, 3.2A
Mary Evans Picture Library: 4.9A, 5.1A, 5.2B
Sonia Halliday Photographs: 4.1A
Michael Holford: 2A, 7E

Imperial War Museum: 5.3A
© Jamie Lawson-Johnston/Pickthall Picture Library: 5.5B
By Permission of the Master and Fellows, Magdelene College, Cambridge: 4.4A
Mansell Collection: 4.5D
Mary Rose Trust: 4.4C
© Max/Pickthall Picture Library: 5.5A
© Mirror Group Newspapers: 5.3C
National Maritime Museum, London: 4.1B, 4.5A, 4.7D
The Board of Trustees of the National Museums and Galleries on Merseyside (Merseyside Maritime Museum): 5.2A
National Portrait Gallery: 8.1B
Peter Newark Pictures: 4.6A
Racal: 7J
The Sutcliffe Gallery, Whitby: 6A, D, E, F, G, H, I, L, M, N, O and P
Syndication International: 4.4B, 4.4D
Ronald Toms/Ace Photo Agency: 6J
© University Museum of National Antiquities, Oslo, Norway: 3.2B
By courtesy of the Board of Trustees of the Victoria and Albert Museum: The Viking Ship Museum, Denmark: 7C, 8.2C
Adam Woolfit/Robert Harding Picture Library: 4.4E, F and G, 4.7A
Zefa: 5.4 A and B, 7G

Cover photograph: The cover illustration shows the *Argo* being equipped. From a 15th-century manuscript in the Bodleian Library, Oxford.

Thanks are also due to Random Century Publishers (The Bodley Head) for permission to reproduce Source 8.1C, taken from *Pugwash and the Fancy-Dress Party* by John Ryan; Cambridge University Press for Source 4.2A, taken from *The First Ships round the World* by Walter Brownlee.

Every effort has been made to contact copyright holders of material reproduced in this book. Any omissions will be rectified in subsequent printings if notice is given to the publisher.

Contents

1	**THE FIRST BOATS**	4
2	**ANCIENT EGYPTIAN AND GREEK SHIPS**	6
3	**BEYOND THE MEDITERRANEAN**	
	3.1 Roman trading ships	10
	3.2 Viking explorers	12
4	**THE AGE OF SAIL**	
	4.1 Lateen sails and caravels	14
	4.2 Magellan's journey round the world	16
	4.3 Life on board ship: the 1500s	18
	4.4 How do we know? The *Mary Rose*	20
	4.5 The Spanish Armada 1588	24
	4.6 The slave trade	26
	4.7 The Battle of Trafalgar 1805	28
	4.8 Life on board ship: emigrant ships	30
	4.9 Clippers	32
5	**STEAM POWER**	
	5.1 The first steamships	34
	5.2 Ocean liners	36
	5.3 The Battle of the Atlantic 1941–43	38
	5.4 Cargo ships	40
	5.5 The end of sail?	42
6	**WHITBY: A 19TH-CENTURY PORT**	44
7	**SAFE PASSAGE: NAVIGATION**	52
8	**AGAINST THE LAW**	
	8.1 Pirates	58
	8.2 Smugglers	60
	8.3 Wreckers	62
	Index	64

1 The first boats

Ten thousand years ago, when people wanted to catch fish from the middle of a river, they sat on a log and floated out to where the fish were. Sometimes they paddled with their hands. Sometimes they used wooden paddles, or poles to push the log along. However, single logs rolled over in the water. Anybody sitting or standing on a log ran the risk of being tipped off. But logs tied together into a **raft** floated well. Rafts were more useful than single logs. A raft could carry more than one person. So one person could paddle and steer while another fished. Rafts could carry people and goods across rivers and even seas.

Source A

People made rafts from bundles of reeds, driftwood or logs. Anything would do, as long as it floated. This carving was made about 2,600 years ago. The fisherman is balancing on an animal skin which has been filled with air so that it will float on water.

The fisherman comes from the ancient land of Assyria. He is probably fishing in the River Tigris. The River Tigris flows through modern Iraq. Assyria was in the north of modern Iraq.

One of the problems with rafts was that they did not keep water out. No matter how tightly the logs were lashed together, water seeped up in between them. Anybody travelling on a raft was bound to get wet, and so were any goods they had with them. People thought of a new way to use logs. They used their stone axes to hollow them out. Sometimes, if the wood was very hard, they burned a hollow out of the log. They made a hollow big enough for one or more people to sit in the log. These were the very first **canoes**. They were made about 8,000 years ago.

People used the materials they found around them to make canoes. The Australian **aborigines** made canoes out of tree bark. First they sewed pieces of eucalyptus tree bark together to make the skin of the canoe. Then they pushed a wooden frame inside the skin to keep the sides apart. The Indians in North America made canoes in the same way. They usually used birch bark. Canoes like this were watertight and light enough to carry easily.

 Source B This aborigine painting shows a man fishing. He is standing in a bark canoe.

Activities

1 **a** Why was a raft better to travel on than a single log? Write down TWO reasons for this.
  b Why was a canoe better to travel on than a raft? Write down TWO reasons for this.

2 Lots of different people in the past built and used rafts and canoes. Copy this table into your book. Fill it in, using what you have read on these pages.

People	Rafts or canoes?
The fisherman in Source A.	
The Australian aborigine in Source B.	
The Indians of North America.	

2 Ancient Egyptian and Greek ships

The first boats used by the Egyptians were probably made out of bundles of **papyrus** reeds, lashed together. The Egyptians used papyrus boats for fishing and for ferrying goods and people up and down the River Nile.

In about 3000 BC the Egyptians began to build wooden ships with square sails and oars. They used sails when the wind would blow them in the right direction, and oars when there was no wind or the wind was blowing the wrong way. These ships meant that Egyptian merchants could leave the River Nile and travel by sea to trade with countries like Palestine and Syria. They also sailed through the Red Sea and down the west coast of Africa.

This painting of an Egyptian ship was made in about 1400 BC.

These are models of papyrus fishing boats. They were put in the tomb of a wealthy Egyptian nobleman, Meket-Re. He lived in Thebes and died in 2000 BC. They were discovered in 1920 by an American archaeologist.

Source C: This picture of a Greek warship was painted in 510 BC. It is painted on a vase.

The ancient Greeks, too, built ships with square sails and oars. They used them for trading and for war. Some of these **galleys** were huge, with rows of oars, one above the other. They were rowed by slaves. It took 1,800 slaves to row the biggest galleys.

Square sails were used on ships in the Mediterranean Sea for thousands of years. Look at the pictures of the Egyptian and Greek square sailed ships (Sources A and C). You will see that the sail hung from a huge **spar** which was attached to the mast high up. The spar and sails could be swung round using the ropes at the bottom of the sail. This meant sailors could move the sail to catch more of the wind. Sailors steered the ship with the large oar at the back (**stern**) of the ship.

Activities

1 Some boats and ships sail faster than others. Copy this table into your book. In the right-hand column write **1** by the fastest ship, **2** by the next fastest and **3** by the slowest.

Boats and ships	Speed
The Greek warship in Source C.	
The Egyptian ship in Source A.	
The fishing boats in Source B.	

2 Write a sentence to explain why you think:
  a the fastest ship was faster than the others.
  b the slowest ship was slower than the others.

7

The Battle of Salamis, 480 BC

One of the very first sea battles we know about is the Battle of Salamis. We know about it because a Greek historian, Herodotus, who was about four years old when it happened, wrote about it years afterwards. So did the Greek poet Aeschylus, who took part in it.

The Persians wanted to destroy the Greeks. A great Persian fleet waited off the coast of Greece. Ahead of them was a narrow **strait** between the island of Salamis and mainland Greece. Somewhere in the strait was the small Greek navy. Persian ships blocked the sea channel on the other side of Salamis. The Greeks could not escape. On the cliffs the Persian King Xerxes watched and waited.

Themistocles, the Greek leader, ordered a single line of Greek galleys to row out of the straits towards the Persians. Three battle lines of Persian warships moved forward to meet them. Suddenly the Greek galleys reversed oars and rowed back into the straits. The Persian ships followed – into a trap. Greek galleys were waiting for them. They rammed and smashed the Persian ships. Then Greek **hoplite** soldiers jumped on board and massacred the Persians. King Xerxes watched in horror as his fleet was destroyed. His dream of conquering Greece was over.

Source D A modern painting of the Battle of Salamis.

Source E

The sea vanished
Under a clogged carpet of shipwrecks,
limbs, bodies,
No sea, and the beaches were cluttered with dead.

Part of the poem written by Aeschylus about the Battle of Salamis.

Activities

1 Look carefully at Source D. The oars were in three rows, one above another. What stopped them getting mixed up with each other?

2 Write a story or draw a big picture about the Battle of Salamis. Use the sources, as well as the writing on these pages, to help you.

How did things change?

1 Put these ships in order of time:

The ship in Source C on page 7
The boats in Source B on page 6
The ships in Source D on page 8

2 What differences can you see between these three sorts of ship? Try to describe the differences as clearly as you can.

3.1 Roman trading ships

Source A

This is a picture of a Roman ship that carried corn. It was painted on a wall in Ostia, a port near Rome, around AD 200. The ship was called *Isis Giminiana* and the captain's name was Farnaces.

The Roman Empire brought peace to the lands around the Mediterranean Sea. This meant that these were good times for trade. Most goods were carried by ships, which kept as close to land as they could so they would not get lost on the open sea. They usually sailed between March and October to avoid winter storms. Even so, many Roman ships were wrecked.

Roman ships carried goods, or **cargo**, from all parts of the Empire to Rome. They carried goods like oil and honey from Greece, corn from Egypt, figs and fishpaste from Spain, cloth from Gaul (France) and tin from Britain. Roman ships carried food, weapons, clothes and money to Roman soldiers wherever they were in the Empire. They carried goods to sell in the cities of the Empire, too. For example, Roman ships brought glass, wine, fine pottery and jewellery to Britain.

Source B

The merchant who overloads his ship must be mad. He piles on the cargo, then sets sail, even when a storm is blowing up. Why does he do it? For money, of course. But before the night is over, the poor fool finds himself in the water, with his purse in his teeth. His ship and cargo are lost.

Written by Juvenal, a Roman poet, in about AD 150.

A map of the sea routes used by Roman trading ships between about 27 BC and AD 410.

Activities

1 Work out how long it might have taken Roman trading ships to sail between:

> Carthage and Ostia
> Rome and Narbo
> Byzantium and Olbia
> Alexandria and Carthage

Use the map and the **Journey times** box on this page to help you.

Here are some examples of the time it took the Romans to travel between these sea ports:

Journey times
Carthage – Narbo	5 days
Ostia – Tarraco	6 days
Ostia – Gades	9 days
Alexandria – Cyrene	6 days

2 Match up the heads and the tails!

Heads
Roman trading ships usually sailed between March and October because…

Some Roman merchants put too much into their ships because…

Roman traders could bring back many different goods because…

Tails
…the Roman Empire was very large.

…they didn't want to be wrecked in winter storms.

…they wanted to make a lot of money.

3.2 Viking explorers

The Vikings were great explorers. They wanted to find new land to settle on; they wanted to trade, and they wanted to raid. Between about AD 700 and 1100 they sailed up rivers deep into Germany, France and Russia. They reached Kiev, Istanbul and Baghdad. They crossed the North Sea to Britain. They sailed to Iceland and then on to Greenland. In about 990 they reached America, which they called Vinland.

The Vikings were able to travel so far because of the ships they built. Viking ships were made out of wood. They were long, slim and light, and had oars as well as sails. Because they were light the ships could be sailed in shallow water and carried between rivers. They could land on beaches and river banks. Viking ships were strong enough to survive storms and did not break up in rough seas.

Source A

This Viking stone was put up by a woman called Estrid in memory of her husband. The writing says 'He visited Jerusalem and died in Greece'.

This map shows Viking trade routes. It shows where they explored by river and sea, the places they went to and the goods they traded.

Source B

Viking leaders and warriors were sometimes buried in their ships when they died. We know a lot about Viking ships because archaeologists have dug some of them up. This Viking ship was excavated at Gokstad in Norway, in 1880.

How did things change?

1 Look carefully at the Roman ship in Source A on page 10 and the Viking ship in Source B on this page.

   Do you think the ships are

   - very alike?
   - quite alike?
   - not at all alike?

   Try to explain why you think this.

2 Look at the map of Viking trade routes on page 12 and the map of Roman trade routes on page 11.

   Did the Viking trading ships go to the same places as Roman trading ships? Explain your answer as carefully as possible.

Activity

Which of these sentences are **true** or **false**? Copy this table into your book. Write **T** or **F** in the middle column. Explain why you think this in the right hand column.

	T or F	Why?
Vikings sailed long distances.		
Viking leaders were sometimes buried in their ships.		
We know very little about Viking ships.		

4.1 Lateen sails and caravels

A thousand years ago Arab traders sailed in the Mediterranean Sea, the Red Sea, the Persian Gulf and the Indian Ocean. They carried goods like rubies, silk, sandalwood, spices and slaves. Their ships had deep **hulls** to carry cargo. The Arabs did not use square sails like the ships of the Romans and Vikings. Square sails worked well when the wind was blowing in the right direction. However, they were difficult to move round if the wind was blowing from the wrong direction, and could make the ship tip over. The Arabs used sails which were shaped like a triangle. These were easy to turn in any direction to catch the wind and sail the ship in the right direction. They were called **lateen sails**.

This picture of Arab traders was painted in 1200s.

Source A

Henry the Navigator (1394–1460) was a Portuguese prince. He wanted Portuguese sailors to explore the coast of Africa and discover a route to the Spice Islands and China. He set up a school of navigation and paid for expeditions. The first expeditions were made in ships with square sails. Then Henry's ship designers built a new type of ship with lateen sails. It was called a **caravel**. It was easy to manoeuvre, and light enough to row. Caravels were ideal for exploring the coast of Africa.

In 1492 **Christopher Columbus** crossed the Atlantic Ocean. He had three ships: the *Pinta*, the *Nina* and the *Santa Maria*. The *Pinta* and the *Nina* were both caravels, but each had a large square sail as well as the lateen sails. Many ships' captains began mixing lateen and square sails.

Activities

1 Draw these ships on a large piece of paper:

   The Egyptian ship in Source A on page 6

   The Arab ship in Source A on page 14

   The caravel in Source B on page 15.

2 **a** Find the **lateen** sails which you have drawn and label them.
   b Find the **square rig** sails which you have drawn and label them.

Source B

A model of a 15th-century caravel with square rig and lateen rig sails.

4.2 Magellan's journey round the world

Source A

No one knows for sure what Magellan's ships were like. By looking at pictures and plans of other ships which were sailing the seas at the same time, historians have been able to work out what Magellan's ship might have looked like. It would have looked something like this drawing.

Source B

He did not tell them everything about the plans for the voyage, because his men might, in amazement and fright, refuse to go with him on so long a voyage.

This was written by Antonio de Pigafetta. He went round the world with Magellan, and wrote down things he saw and did.

Source C

This picture of Seville was painted in the 1500s.

On 20 September 1519 five ships sailed down the river from Seville to the sea. Their sailors thought they were going to make a routine journey across the Atlantic to America. However, their Captain, **Ferdinand Magellan**, planned to go further. He wanted to get to the Spice Islands in the East Indies by sailing west. No one had done this before. The usual way was to sail east. He planned to sail south, following the coast of South America. He hoped he would find a way through to the Pacific Ocean.

It took Magellan 38 days to get through the narrow straits at the southern tip of South America. One ship was wrecked; another turned for home. Three ships got through to the Pacific Ocean. It was emptier and larger than any of the sailors had ever imagined. They ran out of food and water. Many got **scurvy**; some died. Magellan himself was killed by people who lived on one of the islands he visited. His crew later burned one of the ships because there weren't enough people left to sail it. At last, in November 1520, the two remaining ships reached the Spice Islands. There the ships' holds were crammed with spices. They left for Spain. Soon one of the ships began to leak badly and had to turn back.

In September 1522 a battered ship moored in Seville. It was the *Victoria*, the only ship left from Magellan's expedition. Five ships with 234 men had set out; only 18 men and one ship returned. They were the very first to sail right round the world.

Activities

1. Look at Source A. This is what Magellan's ship might have looked like. What sort of ship is it? Is it like:

   - the **caravel** in Source B on page 15?
   - the **Arab ship** in Source A on page 14?

   Explain why you think this.

2. Ask your teacher for an outline map of the world. Use a globe or an atlas to mark on it where Magellan and his ships went.

17

4.3 Life on board ship: the 1500s

Life was hard for sailors 500 years ago. Most of them worked and slept on the open deck. They were burned by the sun, soaked by the sea and rain, and frozen by the winds. Sailors usually had one hot meal a day, which was cooked on deck. Food and drink was stored in the hold of the ship, along with ropes, sails and firewood. Fresh food soon went bad, so the sailors ate that first. Rats and maggots usually got to the rest. The sailors drank water, or water mixed with wine. On long voyages the water went foul and the wine turned to vinegar.

Sailors hardly ever changed their clothes or their boots. Most of them had tiny **lice** crawling over their bodies. They got terrible diseases and many of them died. The disease they got most often was scurvy. No one knew how to prevent it or how to cure it.

Source A We drank water that was yellow and stinking. We had to use sawdust for food, and some of us could not get enough of the rats to eat.

Antonio Pigafetta, who sailed round the world with Magellan, wrote about what happened when they had been at sea for nearly four months.

A ship like the one in Source B could be sailed by about 30 men. The captain divided them into two **watches**. Each watch worked for four hours and then rested for four hours. It was the job of the **ship's boy** to keep an eye on the **sand glass**, which measured the time. He had to call out the time and the change of watches.

Source B This is a modern drawing of a ship in the 1500s. The wooden sides have not been drawn, so that you can see inside the ship.

The job of each watch was to run the ship and to do routine cleaning, mending and repairing. Sailors on watch pumped out sea water, adjusted sails, scrubbed decks, checked the cargo and mended sails and ropes. Some sailors were look-outs. They stood in the **crow's nest** at the top of the mast and shouted out if they saw land, another ship, or any sort of danger. One of the ship's **officers** would then tell the **helmsman**, who was steering the ship with the **tiller**, to change course.

Source C

It rotted all my gums. I cut away the dead flesh and caused much blood to flow. I rinsed my mouth and teeth with urine, rubbing them very hard. I could not eat. I wanted to swallow but could not chew.

A 15th-century sailor describes what it was like to have scurvy.

Activities

1. Look carefully at Source B. Why did crew members have to live and sleep on deck?

2. a What were the **bad** things about life on board ship in the 16th century?
   b What were the **good** things about life on board ship in the 16th century?
   c Make two lists to show these. Which is the longer list – the bad things or the good things?

3. What were these used for on a ship?
   - A sand glass
   - The crow's nest
   - The tiller.

4. Pretend that you are one of the 18 sailors on Magellan's voyage round the world who got back safely. Write a story about the first few days and the last few days of the voyage. Use Sources A, B and C, and the writing on these pages, to help you.

4.4 How do we know? The *Mary Rose*

Source A

The only picture of the *Mary Rose* to survive from the 1500s.

It was 1545. A French fleet was sailing up the English Channel to attack the British navy. King Henry VIII stood watching his ships sail slowly out of Portsmouth harbour to attack. The ships were led by the *Henry Grace à Dieu*, which everyone called 'Great Harry', and the *Mary Rose*. They were the biggest ships in the navy. A few years earlier thay had both been rebuilt. **Gun ports** had been cut in their sides and their guns moved down below the deck. Now they could fire **broadsides** at the enemy. The two fleets moved together, gun ports open, guns at the ready. Suddenly the *Mary Rose* tipped over and slowly sank.

Why had this happened? There were 700 people on board instead of the usual 415. This made the ship difficult to manage. Then the sails were put up badly, and the ship tipped to one side. The sea poured in through the open gun ports. Sailors, archers, pikemen and servants drowned. So did the vice-Admiral, Sir George Carew. Only 35 people survived. No one knew know how to raise the ship. The *Mary Rose*, a fully equipped fighting ship of the 1540s, sank deeper and deeper into soft sand and mud outside Portsmouth harbour.

Archaeologists began working underwater on the *Mary Rose* in 1967. What they found tells us a lot about ships in the 1500s. Everything from the *Mary Rose* was brought to the surface, cleaned, labelled and photographed. In 1982 archaeologists and engineers brought the wooden hull up to the surface.

Source B

A leather bucket.

Source D

An archaeologist makes a sketch of a piece of leather which has been brought up from the sea.

Source E

Source C

A leather shoe. Some shoes were found with foot bones in them.

Gold coins, called angel-nobles.

Source F

A wooden comb in a leather case.

Source G

Bowls, jars, a drug flask and a syringe.

How do we know about the past?

Look at all the sources **except** Source H.

1. Copy the table into your book. Which sources can help you to answer the questions? Write the letter of the source in the middle column, and the answer to the question in the column on the right.

Question	Source	Answer
What did the sailors do in their spare time?		
Was there a doctor on board?		
What sort of guns and shot did they use?		

2. Now write a paragraph describing what the sources tell you about life on the *Mary Rose*.

3. Do these sources tell us everything about life on the *Mary Rose*? If not, what else would you like to know?

Source H — A modern painting showing life aboard the *Mary Rose*.

4.5 The Spanish Armada 1588

King Philip II of Spain wanted to invade England. He ordered a vast fleet of ships to gather in Cadiz harbour. They were to sail for England. Their commander, the Duke of Medina Sidonia, had orders to sail up the English Channel and collect troops from the Netherlands. These troops would be used to invade England.

The Spanish Armada was seen off the coast of Cornwall on 19 July 1588. The ships were sailing close together in a great crescent shape. The strongest ships were on the outside. The English fleet set out from Plymouth after them. The English ships were the same length as the Spanish ships, but the newer ones were not so high in the water. This made them quicker and easier to manoeuvre.

The Armada moved slowly along the English Channel. The English ships attacked when they could, but did no real damage. After nine days the Armada anchored off Calais. It was then the English used fireships. Eight old ships were stuffed full with anything that would burn. Their cannons were loaded and the ships were set alight. They sailed, with no one aboard, straight into the Spanish fleet. There was enormous confusion. The Spanish ships scattered. Then the English attacked. By the end of the day, 800 Spaniards were dead, 3 Spanish ships were sunk and many more badly damaged. The English lost only 50 men and no ships.

Source A

This is part of a chart. It shows the Armada sailing up the English Channel in 1588. It was made by an Englishman, Robert Adams, shortly afterwards.

Source B

The ships were 64 in number, being of a huge size and very stately built and so high they looked like great castles.

An Englishman describes what he saw when he looked at the Armada.

Source C

We could little depend upon the ships that remained, the English fleet being so superior to ours in this sort of fighting because of the strength of their artillery [guns] and the fast sailing of their ships.

Part of a letter from Medina Sidonia, the Spanish commander, to his king, Philip II of Spain.

Source D

The English commander was Lord Howard of Effingham. This picture of his flagship, the *Ark Royal*, was drawn at the time. The ship was new in 1588.

The Armada limped home to Spain. The ships were blown north, around the coast of Scotland, and then south past Ireland. Many ships were wrecked in the terrible winter storms. Altogether 51 ships were lost and 20,000 men killed.

Activity

Copy this table into your book. Find all the reasons you can to explain why the English navy defeated the Spanish Armada. Write the different reasons down in these columns.

Type of ships	Tactics used	Other reasons

4.6 The slave trade

At the beginning of the 1500s, Spanish and Portuguese merchants began shipping black Africans from Africa to America. Once in America, the Africans were made to work as slaves in the sugar, tea and cotton **plantations** on Caribbean islands and in North America. By the 1700s, British merchants did most of the slave trading. Many slave traders became very rich.

Source A

TO BE SOLD on board the Ship *Bance-Ifland*, on tuefday the 6th of *May* next, at *Afhley-Ferry*; a choice cargo of about 250 fine healthy NEGROES, juft arrived from the Windward & Rice Coaft. —The utmoft care has already been taken, and fhall be continued, to keep them free from the leaft danger of being infected with the SMALL-POX, no boat having been on board, and all other communication with people from *Charles-Town* prevented.
Auftin, Laurens, & Appleby.

N. B. Full one Half of the above Negroes have had the SMALL-POX in their own Country.

A 17th-century poster telling people about a newly-arrived cargo of slaves for sale.

Source B A modern painting of a slave ship.

In the 1700s large sailing ships set out for Africa from west coast ports like Bristol, Liverpool and Glasgow. They carried cloth, guns, rum and cheap jewellery. They sailed to **trading posts** on the African coast. They gave the goods they carried to African rulers in exchange for black slaves. Sometimes these slaves were criminals; sometimes they were prisoners from a tribal war; sometimes they were innocent people who had been captured for the slave trade. Ships full of slaves sailed across the Atlantic to the West Indies and America. Many slaves died on the journey. Those who survived were sold to plantation owners. The ships were then loaded with cotton, sugar and tobacco before sailing back to Britain. The whole round trip took between nine months and a year.

Activities

1 Read Source A. Why did it matter so much that these people were healthy?

2 Copy this passage into your book. Use the words underneath to fill in the gaps.

Sailing ships set out from ports like ____ to go to ____. They carried goods like ____ and ____. They gave these to African ____. The ships took ____ over the Atlantic to the ____ ____ and ____. The ships then took goods like ____ and ____ back to Britain.

| rulers cotton slaves Bristol |
| West Indies America sugar |
| guns Africa jewels |

4.7 The Battle of Trafalgar 1805

Napoleon Bonaparte, the ruler of France, tried to take over Europe at the beginning of the 1800s. One of Napoleon's problems was that the British navy was the most powerful in the world. This meant that he couldn't move soldiers and supplies by sea without risking a battle. He couldn't invade Britain until he destroyed the British navy.

For eighteen months the British Mediterranean fleet, commanded by Lord Nelson, had kept the French navy trapped in Toulon harbour. In March 1805 the French ships managed to slip away and joined up with the Spanish navy. Nelson chased them. He finally caught up with them on 21 March off Cape Trafalgar, close to Gibraltar. Both sides got ready for a great sea battle.

Source A

A modern photograph of HMS *Victory* at Portsmouth.

Source B

England expects that every man will do his duty.

This message was sent by Lord Nelson to the British fleet at the beginning of the Battle of Trafalgar. The message was in a special code using flags flown from the mast of his ship, HMS *Victory*.

Source C This diagram shows the position of the most important ships in the British, French and Spanish fleets at the start of the Battle of Trafalgar.

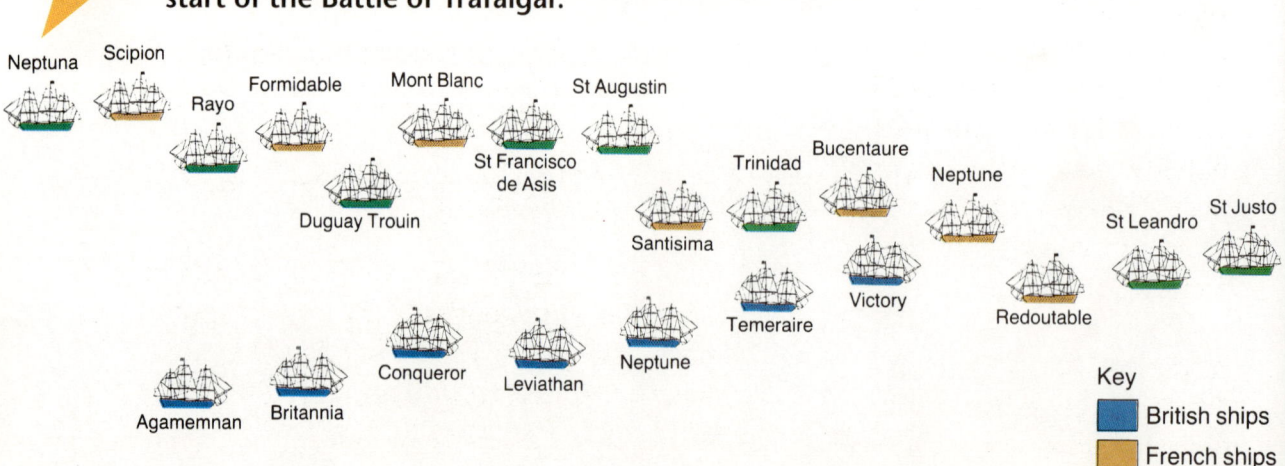

At the command 'Clear for action', men washed decks down and sprinkled them with sand; they rigged up nets to catch falling masts and rigging; they opened gun ports and made the guns ready for action; they filled buckets of water. In ten minutes the British fleet, led by Nelson in his flagship HMS *Victory*, was ready for battle.

Guns blazed, firing from gun ports in the sides of the ships. Cannon balls screamed through the air; sails, masts and rigging fell in tangled masses; rudders and hulls were smashed. The British could fire and reload in 90 seconds. The French and Spanish took much longer. Marksmen, high up in the rigging, fired muskets and threw grenades. The fighting raged for nearly four hours. When the battle ended 23 of the 34 French and Spanish ships were sunk; over 4,000 of their men were killed and 2,000 were wounded. All 27 British ships were still afloat, but 449 men were dead and over 1,000 wounded. Lord Nelson was dead, killed by a French musket ball.

At the end of the Battle of Trafalgar, the British navy controlled the seas.

Source D

A picture of the deck of HMS *Victory* during the Battle of Trafalgar. It was painted by Denis Dighton a few years after the battle.

Activities

Look at Source D.

1. a Which is Admiral Lord Nelson? How do you know?
   b Which are the sailors? How do you know?
   c Which are the soldiers? How do you know?

2. a Write a paragraph describing all the different things which the sailors are doing.
   b Now write a paragraph describing what the soldiers are doing.

3. The artist did not take part in the Battle of Trafalgar. How did he know what to put in his painting? How could we find out whether his painting is accurate or not?

4.8 Life on board ship: emigrant ships

Between 1800 and 1850 over three million men, women and children left the United Kingdom to begin new lives overseas. They travelled by ship to Canada, the USA, South Africa, Australia and New Zealand. Why did they go?

Thousands were driven out of Scotland because the landlords in the Highlands wanted to use the land for sheep farming. Thousands more were desperate to get away from Ireland because the potato crop had failed and people were dying of starvation. People emigrated from England and Wales because they were desperately poor and thought they would have a better life overseas.

The emigrants' lives depended on the captain and crew. It was their job to sail the ship skilfully, to make sure that the ship was kept clean, and to see that the emigrants had enough good food and water. Some voyages were disastrous. Between 1847 and 1853 over 50 emigrant ships were wrecked. Many emigrants fell ill on the journey. In 1852 there was a government enquiry into the ship *Ticonderoga* because 168 out of its 814 passengers died on the journey to Australia.

Source B

We left Plymouth on 7 February and arrived in Melbourne on 6 June. Philip was sick a day or two; John and Isaac were quite at home; Mary, Eliza and Ellen were very well. We had a very good Captain but a very bad doctor. We had six births and seven deaths. We had plenty of food, but the little girls' teeth were not strong enough to eat the biscuits. The water got very bad. The weather came into a calm and we lay just in one place for three weeks. The sailors caught fish and four sharks. We caught sea birds: they were very good for eating. We had one gale then we got into a cold climate.

Part of a letter written to her father by Mrs Phillips who emigrated to Australia in 1849.

Source A

Hundreds of poor people, men, women and children, of all ages from the drivelling idiot of 90 to the babe just born, huddled together, without light, without air, wallowing in filth, sick in body, dispirited in heart.

Part of a letter home from Stephen de Vere, who sailed with Irish emigrants to Canada in 1847.

Activities

1 Look very carefully at Source C.
   a Write a few sentences describing what is happening on the ship.
   b Which parts of the picture did the artist have to find out about, and which parts did the artist make up?

2 What do you think were the worst problems which emigrants faced during their voyage?

Source C A modern painting of emigrants on board ship in the 19th century.

4.9 Clippers

Source A

In 1800 British ships carried more goods than the ships of any other country in the world. Large merchant sailing ships carried goods like wool, tea, coal, sugar, flour and wheat to and from ports in Britain and the rest of the world.

The Americans began building new, fast sailing ships. These ships were designed to cut through the waves instead of riding over them. They were long and narrow, with almost straight sides, flat decks and masses of huge sails. They were called **clippers**. The first American clipper, called the *Ann McKinn*, was built in Baltimore in 1832.

Quickly the British ship owners built clippers too. They did not want the American clippers to take trade away from them. Merchants made a lot of money from trade with India and China, and British ship owners and merchants did not want to lose out. Soon British and American clippers were racing each other along the trade routes to India, China and Australia, with their holds full of tea, wool and the drug opium. In 1865 the *Sir Lancelot*, a British clipper fully laden with tea, took 85 days to sail from Foochow, China, to the Lizard in Cornwall. No ship had done the journey faster.

This picture of the American clipper ship *Antarctic* was painted in 1853.

The End of Clippers

Clippers did not last for long. Some ship builders began to put steam powered engines into the ships they built.

1854   John Elder invented the compound engine. This meant that steamships did not have to carry so much fuel and had more room for cargo.

1869   The Suez Canal was opened. Sailing ships could not use it because of cross-winds and had to go round the Cape of Good Hope to the very south of Africa. This meant that sailing ships had longer journeys to the Far East than steamships, which used the Suez Canal.

1869   The first coast-to-coast railroad was opened in the USA. Goods could be carried by rail from coast to coast instead of having to go by ship around Cape Horn.

1870   Coal depots were set up at Suez, Aden, Singapore and Gibraltar. Steamships carried even less coal than before and had much more room for cargo and passengers.

Were things different then?

1   What are the differences between these ships?

An Arab ship (Source A page 14) and the *Ark Royal* (Source D page 25).
A caravel (Source B page 15) and the *Mary Rose* (Source A page 20).

2   All these ships were used in the 1800s:

Slave ships (page 26)
HMS *Victory* (Source A page 28)
Emigrant ships (page 31)
Clippers (Source A page 32)

Write a paragraph describing the different things which each of these ships did.

5.1 The first steamships

Source A

The *Great Western* arriving in New York harbour on 23 April 1838.

Until the 19th century ships used either wind power (sails) or muscle power (oars) to drive them along. The first ships to be powered by **steam engines** were built in the early 1800s. The steam engines drove large paddle wheels. At first these paddle steamers were used on rivers. Then steamships that could make sea voyages were built. The problem was that for long voyages they had to carry a lot of coal. They had to burn coal to make the steam which drove the engines. This meant that they could not carry much cargo. In 1838 a wooden steamship called the *Great Western* crossed the Atlantic. It used steam power all the way and didn't run out of coal. It was the largest ship ever, and was designed by **I. K. Brunel** and built in Bristol.

Brunel built his second ship, the *Great Britain*, from iron. It was faster than the *Great Western* because he fitted it with a **propeller** instead of paddle wheels. The *Great Britain* was the first iron ship in the world to have a propeller. Iron ships were stronger and lighter than wooden ships. Shipbuilders used iron plates which were 1.5cm thick instead of wooden timbers which were 38cm thick.

From the 1870s ship builders began building ships from steel. This was even lighter and stronger than iron. Twenty years later they began fitting steam **turbine engines** which drove the ships faster and which used less coal. Steamships could then carry more cargo or passengers.

The first steamships burned coal in their boilers to make the steam. Modern ships burn diesel oil to make steam. Some have turbo-electric engines. In these engines, the turbine doesn't drive the propellers directly. Instead, the power from the turbine is used to make electricity. This electricity is stored in batteries. The batteries power electric motors which turn the propellers.

Activities

1 Sort out the words at the end of the sentences.

The *Great Western* steamship was made from	ODOW
The *Great Western* steamship was driven by	LEPADDS
The *Great Britain* steamship was made from	RONI
The *Great Britain* steamship was driven by	LEPROPLERS

2 True or false? Write these sentences into your book. Then decide whether each sentence is true or false. Write **true** beside those which are true and **false** beside those which are false.

The *Great Britain* was slower than the *Great Western*.

The *Great Western* was heavier than the *Great Britain*.

Steel ships were lighter than ships made from iron.

Steam turbine engines used more coal than ordinary steam engines.

5.2 Ocean liners

For hundreds of years ships were used for fighting, fishing, exploring and carrying goods. In the 20th century steamships were specially built to take rich people for holidays and on business trips. These ships were called **liners**. They sailed on regular routes, and were owned by shipping companies called Lines. Liners were like floating hotels. They took people on **cruises** to places like the Caribbean, USA, South America and Africa. People stayed on these liners all the time, and only left them to visit strange and exciting places. Some people travelled by liner to get to where they were going to have their holiday. Rich Europeans and Americans had holidays like this mainly before the First World War (1914–18) and in the 1920s and 1930s.

Source A

This poster, printed in the 1930s, is advertising the White Star Line.

Source B

This picture of the *Titanic* sinking was painted in 1912. People who survived the sinking said that the painting was accurate.

On 10 April 1912, the White Star liner, *Titanic*, left Southampton on her **maiden** voyage. The ship was going to New York with 1,316 passengers and 891 crew. On 14 April the ship's radio operators were told that there was ice in the area. No one thought it was close enough to the *Titanic* to worry about. Just before midnight on 14 April the *Titanic* hit an iceberg. The ship took nearly three hours to sink. There should have been time to save everybody on board. However, the lifeboats only had places for 1,178 people. In the panic and confusion, some lifeboats were never launched, and some were launched only half full. Only 705 people were saved. The rest drowned, trapped in the ship or frozen to death in the sea.

Activities

1 Draw a poster advertising the first voyage of the *Titanic*. Make everything sound grand and exciting! Use Source A, and the writing on page 36, to help you.

2 Write a newspaper article about the sinking of the *Titanic*. Use Source B and the writing on page 37 to help you. You could include an interview with someone who survived. You could also find library books about the *Titanic*, or ask your teacher to tell you more about the disaster.

37

5.3 The Battle of the Atlantic 1941–43

Source A

A photograph of a convoy crossing the Atlantic in 1941.

During the Second World War (1939–45) British and German ships and submarines fought each other, especially in the Atlantic Ocean. The Germans tried to sink ships carrying food and raw materials to Britain. The British tried to keep these ships safe so that they got to British ports with much-needed supplies.

Merchant ships crossed the Atlantic in groups called **convoys**. They were protected by Royal Navy **destroyers** and **corvettes**. German **submarines**, called **U-boats**, attacked convoys. U-boats waited on the surface of the sea. When a U-boat captain saw a convoy, he radioed to other U-boats nearby. The submarines dived and followed the convoy. U-boats usually attacked at night. They fired torpedoes from deep in the sea. The Royal Navy tried to find and destroy U-boats. They destroyed them by dropping **depth charges** which blew the U-boats up. If the U-boats spotted the convoys on the surface, they had time to decide whether to escape or attack.

In March 1943 a pack of 40 U-boats attacked a convoy of 91 ships and sank 21 of them. Only one U-boat was sunk. It looked as if Britain was going to lose the Battle of the Atlantic.

Source B

The only thing that ever really frightened me during the war was the U-boat peril.

Winston Churchill said this after the Second World War. He was the British Prime Minister during the Battle of the Atlantic.

Source C

This picture was printed in a newspaper, the *Daily Mirror*, in 1942. The man who drew the cartoon was trying to tell people that they should think twice before wasting petrol which had been brought across the Atlantic.

"The price of petrol has been increased by one penny"—Official

However, one month later things were very different. New, faster ships, called **frigates**, travelled with the convoys. Long-range aircraft protected convoys for the whole of their voyages. A system called **Huff Duff** (High Frequency Direction Finding) could pick up radio signals between U-boats. The British had cracked the secret code used by German High Command when sending messages to the U-boats. In April 1943, 15 U-boats attacked a slow convoy of 42 British ships. Although the Germans sank 12 ships, this time British ships destroyed 7 U-boats. The next month British ships sank over 41 U-boats.

U-boats carried on sinking ships in the Atlantic until the end of the war. But they were never again such a threat as they were in early 1943.

How did things change?

You will need to look back at pages 8–9, 24–5 and 28–9 before you answer these questions.

1 Copy this timeline into your book:

480 BC   AD 1588   1805   1941–43

Put these battles on the timeline in the right places:
Battle of Trafalgar, Battle of Salamis, Battle of the Atlantic, Spanish Armada.

2 a How did fighting ships change between the Battle of Salamis and the time of the Battle of the Atlantic? List as many changes as you can.
   b Were there any things to do with fighting ships which stayed the same for a long time?

5.4 Cargo ships

Cargo ships carry goods to all parts of the world. They carry goods made in factories, like furniture, cars and televisions; they carry food, like butter, beef and bananas; they carry raw materials like wood and cotton.

Source A

Source B

Container ships carry goods which have already been packed into huge metal containers at the factory. The containers are brought to the docks by lorries and trains. There they are quickly loaded into container ships. Some ships can hold 4,000 containers. Not all the containers will go to the same port. They have to be loaded carefully so that the containers which have to be taken off first are at the top.

A photograph of the British oil tanker, *British Progress*.

Some ships are specially built to carry one sort of cargo, like oil or grain, or goods which will go rotten unless they are kept very cold.

The biggest ships in the world are **oil tankers**. They are built with special tanks in their holds to carry crude oil from oil fields to **refineries**. Some oil tankers are 500 metres long and 70 metres wide. They are far too large to get into ordinary ports and harbours. They anchor out at sea and load and unload their cargo by pumping it along pipelines. Liquid gas and liquid chemicals are carried in tankers built like oil tankers.

Bulk carriers transport cargoes like grain, sand, coal or iron ore. These are poured straight into their holds from the dock. Cargoes like sand and grain are unloaded by being sucked up huge pipes. Lumpy cargoes like coal and iron ore are unloaded by mechanical grabs.

Some cargoes, like butter and meat, would go rotten if they were just carried in an ordinary hold. These cargoes are carried in special **refrigerator ships**. The holds of refrigerator ships are specially made so that they can keep the cargo at the correct low temperature.

A modern container ship being loaded with containers.

Activities

1 What do these cargo ships carry? Copy this table into your book and then fill it in, using these pages to help you.

Type of cargo ship	Goods carried
Refrigerator ships	
Bulk carriers	
Container ships	

2 Look back at pages 10–12. Which of the goods carried by modern cargo ships do you think Roman trading ships might have carried? Copy this list into your book and put a tick (✓) beside the goods which modern AND Roman ships carried.
- Televisions
- Corn
- Crude oil
- Butter
- Cloth
- Cars

5.5 The end of sail?

Source A

Tall ships, like this modern sailing ship, are used nowadays as training ships. Young people spend time living and working on them. They learn all about sailing.

Although steamships took over from sail for trade, this did not mean that people had no more use for sailing boats. Nowadays most sailing boats are used by people for sport. In the early 1900s, only the very rich could afford to sail. Now there are sailing clubs all over the country beside the sea, or by lakes and reservoirs. Many people join clubs and learn to sail. Some sailing ships are small and easily managed; others need large crews. Some yachts race against each other. The most famous races are the Americas Cup, the Whitbread Round the World race and the Fastnet race. Not everyone races. Most people go to sea in their sailing boats just because they enjoy it.

On 27 August 1966 **Francis Chichester** set out from Plymouth. He planned to sail round the world by himself in his yacht *Gipsy Moth IV*. It was a journey of 28,500 miles. Great crowds cheered when, nine months later, he sailed back into Plymouth harbour. The Queen and Prince Philip sent him a 'welcome home' message, and the Prime Minister, Harold Wilson, sent a telegram. Later the Queen made Francis Chichester a knight. He was then called Sir Francis Chichester.

Source B

These yachts are taking part in the Fastnet race in 1991. Most sailing ships today have hulls made out of steel or fibreglass; their sails are made from light, synthetic materials like dacron and nylon.

Activities

1 Look at Sources A and B. Read carefully what the writing underneath them says. They are all about people going to sea in sailing ships in the 20th century. What different reasons can you find for people doing this?

2 Lots of people sailed round the world before Francis Chichester. Why did he want to do this? Why did the Queen make him a knight?

Why did things happen?

1 The ships which you can see in Sources A and B are modern sailing ships. There are lots of different sorts of ships today. Why do people still go to sea in sailing ships?

2 Steamships have changed a lot since the early 1800s. Here are some of the things which helped to bring about changes:

The steam engine was invented in the 1700s.
Good quality iron was made for the first time in the early 1800s.
Sir Charles Parsons invented the steam turbine in 1884.

Write one sentence for each of these, explaining how it helped to change steamships.

3 Steam power made a lot of things possible, or more efficient. Write down as many things as you can find from Units 5.1–5.5, under these headings, which steam power made possible or more efficient.

Trading   Holidays   War

6 Whitby: a 19th-century port

Source A

This photograph of Boulby Bank was taken at the end of the 1800s. Fishermen kept their nets and ropes on the ground floors of the houses. The floors above were lived in by different families, who paid about 1s 3d (6p) rent a week.

The town

Sailors and fishermen did not spend all their time on ships. They lived in houses, cottages and rented rooms in towns and villages close to the sea. They lived in ports like Whitby. Whitby was a busy, bustling port 100 years ago, with a fishing fleet and ship-building yards.

We know a lot about Whitby at that time because a man called Frank Meadow Sutcliffe took photographs of the town and the people who lived there. He took all of the photographs in this unit.

Advertisements from the local newspaper, the *Whitby Times and North Yorkshire Advertiser*, on 7 April 1871.

Source B

WANTED, immediately, APPRENTICES to the Millinery and Dressmaking.—Apply to BLAND & WOMPRA, Whitby.

WANTED, an APPRENTICE to the Confectionary Business.—Apply at HESELTON & ANDREW'S, St. Ann's Staith, Whitby.

TO JET WORKERS.
WANTED a steady man as FOREMAN. To a really practical workman good wages will be given.—Apply *Times* Office.

TO BE LET, with immediate possession, a DWELLING-HOUSE, No. 12, Park-terrace, replete with every convenience.—Apply to CORNER & MARR, Wine Merchants, Whitby.

TO BE LET, and may be entered upon immediately, the old Established PUBLIC-HOUSE, *Crown and Anchor*, Church-street.—Apply H. LINTON, East Row Brewery, Whitby.

TO JET-ORNAMENT MANUFACTURERS, &c.
TO be LET, the TENEMENTS and WORK-SHOP situate in Flowergate, and lately occupied as Gas Office, &c. Very suitable for a Jet-Ornament Manufacturer. For particulars, &c., apply to Mr. A. TODD, Gas Office, Baxtergate, Whitby. Immediate possession can be given.

Source C

HAY FOR SALE.
ABOUT 8 or 9 Tons of first-rate SEED HAY to dispose of.—Apply to BRAIM & SONS.

FOR SALE, the brig "MARY BRACK" 294 tons register, shifts without ballast, and carries tons of coals, or 140 standard of deals, is well found stores.—For particulars apply to Messrs. [...] FOXTON, Whitby.

NOTICE.
FAMILIES who wish to VISIT WHITBY may obtain ELEGANT and COMMODIOUS LODGINGS by applying to Mrs. BRADLEY (West Cliff Lodging-House Agent), Pianoforte Warehouse, News Agent and Circulating Library, 25, Skinner-Whitby.

ROBERT ROBINSON,
COACH BUILDER,
EWISON BANK, BAGDALE, WHITBY.
Carriages and Vehicles built and repaired by the best workmen in a superior style.
First class New Dog Cart, Light Cart, Shooting and other Carriages for Sale.

Advertisements from the local newspaper, the *Whitby Times and North Yorkshire Advertiser*, on 7 April 1871.

Source D

This is a photograph of Whitby Market Place in 1884. Stall-holders paid between 1s 6d (7p) and 2s (10p) each day for their stalls.

Source E

This shop is ready for Christmas! The photograph was taken in about 1900.

Activities

1 Look carefully at Sources A and D. How many things can you find in these photos which tell you that they were taken over 100 years ago?

2 Read Sources B and C. What do these advertisements tell you about the different jobs which Whitby people did?

3 Now look at Sources D and E. Were Whitby people poor or rich? Why do you think this?

Source F

Fishing boats in the harbour at Whitby.

Fishermen

Whitby fishermen caught cod, haddock, plaice, halibut, hake, turbot, herring and mackerel in the North Sea. They caught crabs and lobsters too. In the 1700s and early 1800s some Whitby fishermen hunted whales in the seas around Greenland. Whitby became an important whaling port. Factories in Whitby employed many people to turn the blubber (fat) into oil.

Not all Whitby sailors were fishermen. Some sailors worked in cargo boats carrying goods like wool and coal. A man called James Cook learned about sailing in Whitby. In 1768 he was captain of a Whitby-built ship, the *Endeavour*, which was the first European ship to reach Australia.

Source G

Two fishermen at the Fish Market, Coffee House End, Whitby.

Source H

Fishermen and their crab pots at Whitby. The boy's name is George Walker, and the fisherman on the right is 'Cud' Colley.

Source I

Part of the Cornish fishing fleet moored at Whitby. Every year the Cornish boats caught mackerel and pilchard off the coast of Cornwall, and then sailed north into the Irish Sea for herring. They then went through the Caledonian Canal into the North Sea, and followed the herring south. The Cornish fleet landed lots of herring at Whitby in September and October each year.

Activities

1 Look at Sources F and I.
   a Write down any differences you can find between the boats in the photographs.
   b Write down the things that are the same between the boats.

2 You can see Scottish luggers on the left in Source F. You can see Cornish luggers in Source I. Why did Scottish and Cornish fishermen travel so far to catch fish?

Danger

Going to sea in ships is dangerous. In 1826 Whitby had its first **lifeboat** and lifeboat station. The lifeboatmen had to row their boat through crashing waves and roaring gales to rescue sailors on wrecked ships. In 1861 the lifeboat was called out five times in one day. The lifeboatmen were exhausted. The sixth time they rowed out to sea their boat capsized. They all drowned except Henry Freeman. Twenty years later he was **coxswain** when the men carried their lifeboat overland for six miles through heavy snow drifts. They launched it further up the coast and rescued the crew of a stranded ship.

Source J

A modern lifeboat.

Source K

This is a modern painting of Whitby lifeboatmen rowing to rescue drowning sailors in the 1800s.

Source L

This ship was called the *Mary and Agnes*. It was sailing from Newcastle to London with a cargo of scrap iron. On 24 October 1885 it was caught in a gale off Whitby and wrecked.

Activities

1 How is the lifeboat in Source K different from the modern lifeboat in Source J?

2 The Whitby lifeboat in Source K was very different from a modern one. Are there any things about a lifeboatman's work which have not changed since the end of the 1800s?

3 Make a poster for a sale of goods from the *Mary and Agnes* (Source L).

Fisherwomen

The wives, mothers and sisters of Whitby fishermen didn't go to sea. They worked hard on land. They collected bait; they made and mended nets; they knitted and made lace; they sold fish in the fish market. On top of all this they washed and scrubbed, cooked and cleaned, sewed and mended and did everything they could to look after their families.

Source M

These women are going to gather limpets from the rocks on the beach. They can only go at low tide when the rocks are uncovered. Their husbands, fathers and sons are fishermen. They use the limpets as bait on their fishing lines.

Source N

One of these women is making lace. The other one is knitting a gansey pattern fisherman's sweater. Every fishing port had its own special gansey pattern.

Source O

These women are mending fishing nets.

50

Source P

This is the New Quay fish stall in Whitby. The man with the cap is called Tom Gaines. He fished for herring. Nell Bakehouse is in the middle of the photograph. She is talking to Eleanor Locker.

Activity

Look at all the photographs on pages 50 and 51. What are the women doing? Copy this table into your book. Put the letters of the sources which show you these activities in the column on the right.

What are they doing?	Source
Selling fish	
Making lace	
Mending nets	
Gathering limpets	
Knitting	

How do we know about the past?

1. Look back at all the photographs of Whitby on pages 44–51.

   Which of the photographs would you use to show that
   - Some Whitby people had the money to buy lots of different sorts of food
   - Fisherwomen in Whitby did lots of different jobs
   - Fishing boats came to Whitby from other parts of Britain
   - Fishing was a dangerous job.

2. Use all the sources on pages 44–51 to help you to write about life in Whitby in the late 1800s. Try to write about as many different things as you can.

3. Did you find any of the sources more useful than others? Which ones, and why? Were any of the sources not useful at all? Explain why not.

7 Safe passage: navigation

Viking navigation

There are lots of ways in which ships can be wrecked and seafarers drowned. During a war, enemies deliberately destroyed each other's ships. Sometimes gales and hurricanes drive ships on to rocks or swamp them with huge waves. However, most disasters happen because the ship's crew can't work out exactly where they are. They hit rocks or run aground in unknown waters. The aim of all captains and all seafarers has always been the same: to finish a voyage safely. This is called **safe passage**. Navigation helps seafarers to make sure they have safe passage.

The Vikings knew their coastline and rocky inlets well. They knew where there were hidden rocks and dangerous currents. It was different when they crossed the North Sea to Britain, Iceland and Greenland. They could not see a coastline for many days. How did they find their way across the open sea? No one knows for sure. It is likely that during the day they used the sun to steer by, and at night they used the stars. We know this because the Vikings have left us some clues.

Source A From Hernar keep sailing west to Hvarf. Sail north of Shetland so you just see it in very clear weather, but south of the Faroes so the sea appears halfway up the mountains. Then south of Iceland so you see the birds and whales from there.

These instructions explain how to get from Norway to Greenland. They are from a Viking book, the Landnamabok.

Source B This is a modern picture of a Viking boat. The artist used photographs of excavations like Source C on page 13 so that the picture would be as realistic as possible.

Source C

Archaeologists found the broken piece of wood (on the right) in a ruined Viking village in Greenland. The archaeologists think it was once part of a bearing dial. They think Viking bearing dials were like the drawing on the left. The dial was marked with compass points. The Vikings used the bearing dial to keep them on course when they were sailing in open seas.

Activity

Vikings faced a lot of problems when they left their own coasts and crossed the North Sea. They could avoid some of these if they were good at navigation. They could do nothing about others. Copy this table into your book and fill it in. Use the writing on these pages to help you.

Problem	How could they avoid this?
Gales and hurricanes	
Hitting hidden rocks	
Losing their way during the day	
Losing their way at night	

Navigation in the 1500s

Sailors had to be able to work out where their ship was, and plot a course to bring them safely to where they wanted to be.

Sailors needed to work out how fast their ship was travelling. They tied knots at regular intervals along a piece of rope, and then they tied the rope to a log of wood. They threw the log over the side of the ship. A sailor used a sand glass to time the speed at which the knots ran through his hand. This way sailors could work out how fast they were sailing, and how far. Sailors also needed to know in which direction they were sailing. To do this they used navigational instruments.

Source D

This picture shows a Portuguese navigator using a cross-staff. These helped sailors work out how far north, or south, of the equator they were.

Source E

This compass was used in the 1500s. It showed the helmsman whether he was steering north, south, east or west.

Navigators made charts of the seas and coastlines. These were very valuable, because the success or failure of a voyage could depend upon how accurate they were.

Source F

This map, showing the coastline of the Mediterranean Sea, was made in the 1500s.

Activities

1 What did sailors in the 1500s use
   - To find out where they were?
   - To plan where they were going?
   - To find out in which direction they were sailing?
   - To find out how far they had travelled?

2 How do you think Source F would help sailors to navigate?

Navigation today

Sailors today still need to know exactly where their ship is in the sea. Navigators work out the route their ship is going to take. They use maps and charts and scientific and electronic instruments.

Some navigators use a radio called a **direction finder**. This picks up signals from radio transmitters on land, and records the direction of each signal. The navigator knows where these transmitters are, and so can work out where the ship is.

Some ships can pick up signals from **satellites**. Ships can pick up these signals wherever they are in the world. Navigating officers then work out the exact position of their ship.

Source G

This navigator is using a **sextant**. This measures the angle between the horizon and the sun or a star. He will then use a **chronometer** to tell him the exact time, and a compass to tell him the direction of the sun. He will put all this data together and use special tables to give him the exact position of his ship.

Source H

This navigator is putting his ship's position on a chart.

Source I

Source J

The **radar scanner** goes round and round on top of the mast. It sends out **radio waves**. When the radio waves hit something solid, like a cliff or another ship, they bounce back to the scanner. These waves are changed into signals which can be seen on a screen. The radio officer and the navigation officer can see at once whether there is anything solid within 60km of their ship. In the same way **echo sounders** bounce sound waves down to the sea bed. Navigators can work out how much water there is underneath the ship.

Activities

1 What do sailors today use
   - To find out where they are?
   - To plan where they are going?
   - To find out in which direction they are sailing?
   - To find out how far they have travelled?

2 Are any of the instruments which modern sailors use like those used in the 1500s? Which ones are different? How are they different?

How have things changed?

Look back at pages 12–13 and 18–25 before you answer the questions.

1 Why was navigation better and safer in the 1500s than for the Vikings?

2 Why is navigation better and safer today than in the 1500s?

3 Which of these was made possible by better navigational aids?
   Sailing across open seas.
   Avoiding rocks and dangerous currents.
   Working out how fast the ship is going.
   Finding out how much cargo the ship is carrying.
   Working out exactly where the ship is going.
   Finding out the name of the captain of the ship.

Now write beside each of these the modern instrument which has made it possible.

8.1 Pirates

Pirates have sailed the seas of the world ever since the first ships carried cargo. Pirates are sea robbers. They rob ships of the goods they are carrying. Sometimes they steal the ship, too.

Pirates are criminals. From the 1500s to the 1700s, if British pirates were caught and found guilty, they were hanged from Execution Dock at Wapping, London. Their bodies were then chained up along the banks of the River Thames as an awful warning to others. Today, people found guilty of being pirates are sent to prison for a long time.

The best years for pirates were between 1550 and 1750. A sea route to India had been discovered and America was being explored by Europeans. Hundreds of ships sailed the seas to Europe. They were laden with spices, silks, gold, silver and tobacco. What a wonderful opportunity for pirates!

Source A

This picture is of a pirate called Edward Teach. His nickname was 'Blackbeard'. Teach and his pirate crew attacked trading ships off the coast of North America at the beginning of the 1700s. He **smuggled** the stolen goods ashore and sold them.

Source B

This portrait of Francis Drake was painted in the 1500s. He was a special kind of pirate. Queen Elizabeth I knew exactly what he was doing when he attacked Spanish galleons and captured their cargoes of silver, silks and spices. She called him 'My little pirate'. She gave him documents called 'Letters of Marque' which kept him safe from English law. In return Francis Drake had to share everything he captured with the Queen.

Francis Drake and 'Blackbeard' were two very famous pirates. There have been lots of others. In the 1500s Arouj Barbarossa and his brother Khery-ed-Din led pirate gangs from north Africa and Turkey. They were protected by the King of Tunis and shared their booty with him. The Barbarossa brothers attacked European ships sailing in the Mediterranean, including two treasure ships belonging to the Pope.

Bartholomew Roberts seems to have been the most successful pirate ever. He worked in the Caribbean Sea and off the coasts of west Africa and Canada. Between 1720 and 1722 he captured more than 400 ships. He should have ended up very rich indeed, but in 1722 he was shot in the throat during a battle with an English warship and died.

Shap-'ng-Tsai was a Chinese pirate. He controlled a large pirate fleet in the China Sea for many years. In 1849 his fleet was finally cornered by British ships in the Gulf of Tonkin. The pirate fleet was destroyed, but Shap escaped. He was given a pardon by the Chinese authorities.

There were women pirates, too. Anne Bonney and Mary Read joined the crew of a pirate captain, John Rackham. In 1720 their ship was attacked off Jamaica. Anne and Mary were the last pirates left fighting on deck. All the men were dead or hiding below.

Source C

Some pirates are made up. You can read about these imaginary pirates in books and comics, or watch them on TV or at the cinema. This picture is on the front of a book about an imaginary pirate called Captain Pugwash. John Ryan wrote the book.

Activity

Which of these pirates really lived? Which are imaginary?
- Blackbeard
- Francis Drake
- Shap-'ng Tsai
- Mary Read
- Captain Pugwash

8.2 Smugglers

In the 1700s and 1800s the government put taxes (called **duty**) on a lot of goods that were imported into England. They put duty on things like brandy, lace, tobacco and tea. **Smugglers** bought these things in Europe. Then, they brought them secretly into England by ship. They sold them quietly to their customers without charging duty. Anything with a high duty was worth smuggling. The smugglers made a profit, and people paid less than they would have done in the shops. However, smuggling was a crime. The government was cheated out of tax, and customs officers did their best to catch the smugglers. Smuggling is still a crime today.

Often whole villages were involved in smuggling. There was money to be made for everyone. In some places the local solicitor gave the cash to set up the smugglers' gang. In some villages the school teacher kept the smugglers' accounts. Sometimes the vicar helped store the **contraband** (smuggled goods). Can you think how fishermen, stagecoach drivers, shopkeepers and farmworkers could help too? Some smugglers built secret tunnels from farms, inns and churches down to the beach so that they could move the contraband without being seen. They built special hiding places in tombs and pulpits, and made false walls and ceilings in houses. The magistrates were meant to punish smugglers who were caught. Sometimes the magistrates were smugglers themselves.

Source A

The ship *Five Brothers* and the ship's captain, William Masters, were seized by Customs officers. They found, hidden in the bed-places and under the sails, 126 bales containing 3,131 lbs of tobacco and 6 bales of tobacco stems, weighing 178 lbs. Mr Potbury, a Customs officer, told the Court that the duty on the tobacco found in the ship was £1,510 19s. The Captain said he knew to whom he should have delivered the tobacco, but refused to tell their names. All he would say was that they did not live very far away. He was sent to Devon County Goal for nine months.

This is from a report in a newspaper, the *Exeter Flying Post*, on 2 September 1841.

Source B

Andrews the smuggler, brought this night, about 11 o'clock, a bag of Hyson tea, 6 pound in weight. He frightened us a little by whistling under the Parlour window just as we were going to bed. I paid him for the tea at 10s 6d a pound.

Parson Woodforde wrote this in his diary on 29 March 1777. At the time shops sold Hyson tea for 15s a pound.

Source C

This picture of smugglers was painted in the 1900s by W. B. Wollen.

When the ship carrying contraband was near the shore, the **spotsman** would check that no customs men were near. Then he would signal to the ship with a lantern or flares. During daytime a different signal would be arranged. At the signal, the contraband would be lowered into small boats and rowed ashore. **Bat-men**, armed with staves and cudgels, guarded the men who unloaded the cargo, just in case customs men were hiding close by. Carts stood ready to take the goods away to a safe hiding place. The contraband was then secretly taken to customers. Sometimes the smugglers took silk and tea in carts, hidden under turfs and logs. Sometimes women smugglers poured brandy into pigs' bladders and hid them under their skirts. Can you think of other ways of making secret deliveries?

Activities

1 Why did people want to be smugglers?

2 How do you think fishermen, stagecoach drivers, shopkeepers and farmers could help the smugglers?

3 Write a story, or paint a picture, about smugglers. Make it as exciting as you can, **but** – it must be right! Use the writing and the sources on pages 60–1 to help you.

8.3 Wreckers

In some places **wreckers** set out to destroy ships and steal cargo. They did not care how many sailors drowned. Wreckers waited until they knew a cargo ship was due to sail close to the shore. They hid and waited for the night. Then they flashed lights at the ship. They tried to trick the ship's captain into thinking the lights showed a safe way into harbour. In this way the wreckers lured ships onto rocks where they broke up. The cargo spilled into the sea and was washed ashore. The wreckers grabbed what they could. Sometimes they robbed the bodies of drowned seamen. Then, like the smugglers, they sold what they had obtained. Wreckers, however, didn't always know what cargo would be washed ashore when they wrecked a ship. They must have had some surprises!

Activity

Look back at pages 60–1. How were wreckers different from smugglers?

What do people say about the past?

Read what these people are saying about smugglers.

A: *Smugglers were wicked. They brought goods like French brandy into England without paying any duties.*

B: *Smugglers were heroes. They wanted to help people.*

1 Are they saying the same things about smugglers?

2 Find:
  - one **fact** in what person A is saying
  - one **point of view** in what person A is saying.

Can you find any points of view in what person B is saying?
Can you find any facts in what person B is saying?

3 'People were always pleased when a pirate or a smuggler was caught.' Do you agree? Use what you have learned from pages 58–62 to help you answer.

Index

aborigines 5
Africa 15, 26, 27, 36
America 12, 17, 26, 27, 58
Assyria 4
Atlantic Ocean 15, 17, 27, 34, 38, 39
Australia 30, 32, 46

Baghdad 12
Battle of: Salamis 8, 9
   the Atlantic 38, 39
   Trafalgar 27, 28, 29, 30
Bristol 27
Brunel, I. K. 34
bulk carriers 41

Canada 30, 59
canoes 5
caravels 15
cargo ships: Arab 14
   Egyptian 6
   Roman 10, 11
Caribbean 26, 36, 59
charts 55
Chichester, Francis 42
China 15, 32, 59
clippers 32, 33
Columbus, Christopher 15
compass 54
container ships 40
convoys 38, 39
cross-staff 54
crow's nest 19
cruises 36

Drake, Francis 58

East Indies 17
echo sounder 57
Egypt 10
Egyptians 6, 7
English Channel 20, 24

fishermen 4, 44, 46, 47
France 12

galleys 7
Gaul 10

Germany 12
Gibraltar 28
Glasgow 27
Greece 8, 10
Greeks 7, 8
Greenland 12, 46, 52

helmsman 19
Henry the Navigator 15

Iceland 12, 52
Indian Ocean 14
India 32
Istanbul 12

Kiev 12
King Henry VIII 20
King Philip II of Spain 24
King Xerxes of Persia 8

lifeboat 48
lifeboatmen 48
liners 36
Liverpool 27
Lord Nelson 28, 29

Magellan, Ferdinand 16, 17, 18
Mediterranean Sea 7, 10, 14

Napoleon Bonaparte 28
New Zealand 30
North Sea 12, 47, 52
Norway 12

oars 6, 7, 12
oil tankers 41

Pacific Ocean 17
paddles 4
paddle steamers 34
paddle wheels 34
Palestine 6
papyrus 6
Persian Gulf 14
Persians 8
plantations 26
Portsmouth 20
propeller 35

Queen Elizabeth I 58

radar scanner 57
raft 4, 5
Red Sea 6, 14
refrigerator ships 41
River Nile 6
Rome 10
Russia 12

sailing clubs 42
sails: lateen 14, 15
   square 6, 7, 14, 15
sand glass 18
scurvy 17, 18
Seville 17
sextant 56
ships: *Ann McKinn* 32
   Ark Royal 25
   British Progress 40
   Endeavour 46
   Isis Giminiana 10
   Gipsy Moth IV 42
   Great Britain 35
   Great Western 34
   Mary and Agnes 48
   Nina 15
   Pinta 15
   Santa Maria 15
   Ticonderoga 30
   Titanic 37
   Victory 28, 29
slaves 26, 27
South Africa 30
South America 17, 36
Spain 10, 17, 25
Spanish Armada 24, 25
Spice Islands 15, 17
steam engines 34

tiller 19
traders: Arab 14
   slave 26
turbine 35

U-boats 38, 39
USA 30, 36

Vikings 12, 52, 53

West Indies 27